CU00704210

YEAR AT GLANCE

January

S	M	T	W	T	F	S
						1
2	3	4	5	6	7	8
9	10	11	12	13	14	15
16	17	18	19	20	21	22
23	24	25	26	27	28	29
30	31					

February

S	M	T	W	T	F	S
		1	2	3	4	5
6	7	8	9	10	11	12
13	14	15	16	17	18	19
20	21	22	23	24	25	26
27	28					

March

S	M	T	W	T	F	S
		1	2	3	4	5
6	7	8	9	10	11	12
13	14	15	16	17	18	19
20	21	22	23	24	25	26
27	28	29	30	31		

April

S	M	T	W	T	F	S
					1	2
3	4	5	6	7	8	9
10	11	12	13	14	15	16
17	18	19	20	21	22	23
24	25	26	27	28	29	30

May

S	M	T	W	T	F	S
1	2	3	4	5	6	7
8	9	10	11	12	13	14
15	16	17	18	19	20	21
22	23	24	25	26	27	28
29	30	31				

June

S	M	T	W	T	F	S
			1	2	3	4
5	6	7	8	9	10	11
12	13	14	15	16	17	18
19	20	21	22	23	24	25
26	27	28	29	30		

July

S	M	T	W	T	F	S
					1	2
3	4	5	6	7	8	9
10	11	12	13	14	15	16
17	18	19	20	21	22	23
24	25	26	27	28	29	30
31						

August

S	M	T	W	T	F	S
	1	2	3	4	5	6
7	8	9	10	11	12	13
14	15	16	17	18	19	20
21	22	23	24	25	26	27
28	29	30	31			

September

S	M	T	W	T	F	S
				1	2	3
4	5	6	7	8	9	10
11	12	13	14	15	16	17
18	19	20	21	22	23	24
25	26	27	28	29	30	

October

S	M	T	W	T	F	S
						1
2	3	4	5	6	7	8
9	10	11	12	13	14	15
16	17	18	19	20	21	22
23	24	25	26	27	28	29
30	31					

November

S	M	T	W	T	F	S
		1	2	3	4	5
6	7	8	9	10	11	12
13	14	15	16	17	18	19
20	21	22	23	24	25	26
27	28	29	30			

December

S	M	T	W	T	F	S
				1	2	3
4	5	6	7	8	9	10
11	12	13	14	15	16	17
18	19	20	21	22	23	24
25	26	27	28	29	30	31

MONTHLY PLANNER

Jan	Feb	Mar

Apr	May	Jun

Jul	Aug	Sep

Oct	Nov	Dec

Notes :

NOTES

Sun Mon Tue Wed Thu Fri Sat

WEEKLY PLANNER

MON	TUE	WED	THU	FRI	SAT	SUN

GOALS

NOTES

DAILY

WEEKLY FOCUS	NOTES

Sunday

Monday

Tuesday

Wednesday

Thursday

Friday

Saturday

DAILY

WEEKLY FOCUS

NOTES

Sunday

Monday

Tuesday

Wednesday

Thursday

Friday

Saturday

DAILY

WEEKLY FOCUS

NOTES

Sunday

Monday

Tuesday

Wednesday

Thursday

Friday

Saturday

DAILY

WEEKLY FOCUS

NOTES

Sunday

Monday

Tuesday

Wednesday

Thursday

Friday

Saturday

WEEKLY PLANNER

MON	TUE	WED	THU	FRI	SAT	SUN

GOALS

NOTES

DAILY

WEEKLY FOCUS

NOTES

Sunday

Monday

Tuesday

Wednesday

Thursday

Friday

Saturday

DAILY

WEEKLY FOCUS

NOTES

Sunday

Monday

Tuesday

Wednesday

Thursday

Friday

Saturday

DAILY

WEEKLY FOCUS	NOTES

Sunday

Monday

Tuesday

Wednesday

Thursday

Friday

Saturday

DAILY

WEEKLY FOCUS	NOTES

Sunday

Monday

Tuesday

Wednesday

Thursday

Friday

Saturday

Sun Mon Tue Wed Thu Fri Sat

WEEKLY PLANNER

MON	TUE	WED	THU	FRI	SAT	SUN

GOALS

NOTES

DAILY

WEEKLY FOCUS

NOTES

Sunday

Monday

Tuesday

Wednesday

Thursday

Friday

Saturday

DAILY

WEEKLY FOCUS

NOTES

Sunday

Monday

Tuesday

Wednesday

Thursday

Friday

Saturday

DAILY

WEEKLY FOCUS	NOTES

Sunday

Monday | **Tuesday**

Wednesday | **Thursday**

Friday | **Saturday**

DAILY

WEEKLY FOCUS

NOTES

Sunday

Monday

Tuesday

Wednesday

Thursday

Friday

Saturday

WEEKLY PLANNER

MON	TUE	WED	THU	FRI	SAT	SUN

GOALS

NOTES

DAILY

WEEKLY FOCUS

NOTES

Sunday

Monday

Tuesday

Wednesday

Thursday

Friday

Saturday

DAILY

WEEKLY FOCUS

NOTES

Sunday

Monday

Tuesday

Wednesday

Thursday

Friday

Saturday

DAILY

WEEKLY FOCUS

NOTES

Sunday

Monday

Tuesday

Wednesday

Thursday

Friday

Saturday

DAILY

WEEKLY FOCUS

NOTES

Sunday

Monday

Tuesday

Wednesday

Thursday

Friday

Saturday

Sun Mon Tue Wed Thu Fri Sat

WEEKLY PLANNER

MON	TUE	WED	THU	FRI	SAT	SUN

GOALS

NOTES

DAILY

WEEKLY FOCUS	NOTES

Sunday

_____
_____
_____
_____
_____

Monday

_____
_____
_____
_____
_____

Tuesday

_____
_____
_____
_____
_____

Wednesday

_____
_____
_____
_____
_____

Thursday

_____
_____
_____
_____
_____

Friday

_____
_____
_____
_____
_____

Saturday

_____
_____
_____
_____
_____

DAILY

WEEKLY FOCUS

NOTES

Sunday

Monday

Tuesday

Wednesday

Thursday

Friday

Saturday

DAILY

WEEKLY FOCUS

NOTES

Sunday

Monday

Tuesday

Wednesday

Thursday

Friday

Saturday

DAILY

WEEKLY FOCUS

NOTES

Sunday

Monday

Tuesday

Wednesday

Thursday

Friday

Saturday

WEEKLY PLANNER

MON	TUE	WED	THU	FRI	SAT	SUN

GOALS

NOTES

DAILY

WEEKLY FOCUS

NOTES

Sunday

Monday

Tuesday

Wednesday

Thursday

Friday

Saturday

DAILY

WEEKLY FOCUS

NOTES

Sunday

Monday

Tuesday

Wednesday

Thursday

Friday

Saturday

DAILY

WEEKLY FOCUS

NOTES

Sunday

- _____
- _____
- _____
- _____
- _____

Monday

- _____
- _____
- _____
- _____
- _____

Tuesday

- _____
- _____
- _____
- _____
- _____

Wednesday

- _____
- _____
- _____
- _____
- _____

Thursday

- _____
- _____
- _____
- _____
- _____

Friday

- _____
- _____
- _____
- _____
- _____

Saturday

- _____
- _____
- _____
- _____
- _____

DAILY

WEEKLY FOCUS

NOTES

Sunday

Monday

Tuesday

Wednesday

Thursday

Friday

Saturday

WEEKLY PLANNER

MON	TUE	WED	THU	FRI	SAT	SUN

GOALS

NOTES

DAILY

WEEKLY FOCUS

NOTES

Sunday

Monday

Tuesday

Wednesday

Thursday

Friday

Saturday

DAILY

WEEKLY FOCUS

NOTES

Sunday

Monday

Tuesday

Wednesday

Thursday

Friday

Saturday

DAILY

WEEKLY FOCUS

NOTES

Sunday

Monday

Tuesday

Wednesday

Thursday

Friday

Saturday

DAILY

Week 1 / 2 / 3 / 4

WEEKLY FOCUS

NOTES

Sunday

Monday

Tuesday

Wednesday

Thursday

Friday

Saturday

Sun Mon Tue Wed Thu Fri Sat

WEEKLY PLANNER

MON	TUE	WED	THU	FRI	SAT	SUN

GOALS

NOTES

DAILY

WEEKLY FOCUS

NOTES

Sunday

Monday

Tuesday

Wednesday

Thursday

Friday

Saturday

DAILY

Week 1 / 2 / 3 / 4

WEEKLY FOCUS

NOTES

Sunday

Monday

Tuesday

Wednesday

Thursday

Friday

Saturday

DAILY

WEEKLY FOCUS

NOTES

Sunday

Monday

Tuesday

Wednesday

Thursday

Friday

Saturday

DAILY

WEEKLY FOCUS

NOTES

Sunday

- _____
- _____
- _____
- _____
- _____

Monday

- _____
- _____
- _____
- _____
- _____

Tuesday

- _____
- _____
- _____
- _____
- _____

Wednesday

- _____
- _____
- _____
- _____
- _____

Thursday

- _____
- _____
- _____
- _____
- _____

Friday

- _____
- _____
- _____
- _____
- _____

Saturday

- _____
- _____
- _____
- _____
- _____

WEEKLY
PLANNER

MON	TUE	WED	THU	FRI	SAT	SUN

GOALS

NOTES

DAILY

WEEKLY FOCUS

NOTES

Sunday

Monday

Tuesday

Wednesday

Thursday

Friday

Saturday

DAILY

WEEKLY FOCUS

NOTES

Sunday

Monday

Tuesday

Wednesday

Thursday

Friday

Saturday

DAILY

WEEKLY FOCUS

NOTES

Sunday

Monday

Tuesday

Wednesday

Thursday

Friday

Saturday

DAILY

WEEKLY FOCUS

NOTES

Sunday

Monday

Tuesday

Wednesday

Thursday

Friday

Saturday

WEEKLY PLANNER

MON	TUE	WED	THU	FRI	SAT	SUN

GOALS

NOTES

DAILY

WEEKLY FOCUS

NOTES

Sunday

Monday

Tuesday

Wednesday

Thursday

Friday

Saturday

DAILY

WEEKLY FOCUS

NOTES

Sunday

Monday

Tuesday

Wednesday

Thursday

Friday

Saturday

DAILY

WEEKLY FOCUS

NOTES

Sunday

- _____
- _____
- _____
- _____
- _____

Monday

- _____
- _____
- _____
- _____
- _____

Tuesday

- _____
- _____
- _____
- _____
- _____

Wednesday

- _____
- _____
- _____
- _____
- _____

Thursday

- _____
- _____
- _____
- _____
- _____

Friday

- _____
- _____
- _____
- _____
- _____

Saturday

- _____
- _____
- _____
- _____
- _____

DAILY

WEEKLY FOCUS

NOTES

Sunday

Monday

Tuesday

Wednesday

Thursday

Friday

Saturday

Sun Mon Tue Wed Thu Fri Sat

WEEKLY PLANNER

MON	TUE	WED	THU	FRI	SAT	SUN

GOALS

NOTES

DAILY

WEEKLY FOCUS

NOTES

Sunday

Monday

Tuesday

Wednesday

Thursday

Friday

Saturday

DAILY

WEEKLY FOCUS

NOTES

Sunday

Monday

Tuesday

Wednesday

Thursday

Friday

Saturday

DAILY

WEEKLY FOCUS

NOTES

Sunday

Monday

Tuesday

Wednesday

Thursday

Friday

Saturday

DAILY

WEEKLY FOCUS

NOTES

Sunday

Monday

Tuesday

Wednesday

Thursday

Friday

Saturday

WEEKLY
PLANNER

MON	TUE	WED	THU	FRI	SAT	SUN

GOALS

NOTES

DAILY

WEEKLY FOCUS

NOTES

Sunday

Monday

Tuesday

Wednesday

Thursday

Friday

Saturday

DAILY

WEEKLY FOCUS

NOTES

Sunday

Monday

Tuesday

Wednesday

Thursday

Friday

Saturday

DAILY

WEEKLY FOCUS

NOTES

Sunday

Monday

Tuesday

Wednesday

Thursday

Friday

Saturday

DAILY

WEEKLY FOCUS

NOTES

Sunday

Monday

Tuesday

Wednesday

Thursday

Friday

Saturday

NOTES

NOTES

NOTES

NOTES

NOTES

NOTES

NOTES

NOTES

NOTES

NOTES

NOTES

NOTES

NOTES

NOTES

NOTES

NOTES

NOTES

NOTES

NOTES

NOTES

NOTES

NOTES

NOTES

NOTES

NOTES

NOTES

NOTES

NOTES

NOTES

NOTES

NOTES

NOTES

NOTES

NOTES

NOTES

NOTES

NOTES

NOTES

NOTES

NOTES

NOTES

NOTES

NOTES

NOTES

NOTES

Printed in Great Britain
by Amazon